CHINA

the culture

Bobbie Kalman

The Lands, Peoples, and Cultures Series

Crabtree Publishing Company

The Lands, Peoples, and Cultures Series
Created by Bobbie Kalman

Writing team
Bobbie Kalman
Margaret Hoogeveen
Christine Arthurs

Editor-in-Chief
Bobbie Kalman

Editors
Janine Schaub
Christine Arthurs
Margaret Hoogeveen

Research
Margaret Hoogeveen
Moira Daly
Virginia Neale

Design and layout
Heather Delfino
Margaret Hoogeveen

Printer
Worzalla Publishing Company
Stevens Point, Wisconsin

Illustrations
Halina Below-Spada p. 6, 18, 30
Tina Holdcroft p. 24-25
Greg Ruhl p. 22
Janet Wilson p. 23
Zhang Furong p. 4

Photography acknowledgments
Cover shot: Ken Ginn
Jim Bryant: p. 10(left and right), 11(right), 15(right), 29; Beverly Deutsch: p. 4, 12(top left);
Judy Davies: p. 27(circle); Ken Ginn: Title page, p. 31; Ivanka Lupenic: p. 5(top right), 14(left), 15(left), 21(inset);
Ruth Malloy: p.17(top), 28(bottom); Pat Morrow/First Light: p. 5(top left), 12(top right), 20, 21(top), 28(top);
Christine McClymont: p. 8(bottom right); Gayle McDougall: p. 7(bottom two), p.8(top), 17(circle);
Courtesy of the Consulate General of the People's Republic of China: p. 22; Courtesy of the
Royal Ontario Museum: p. 7(top two), 9, 27(top right); Larry Rossignol: p. 5(bottom), 12(bottom);
Caroline Walker: p. 8(bottom left), 14(right), 18, 27(bottom); Zhao Meichang: p. 16.

For my aunt Margaret

Cataloguing in Publication Data

Kalman, Bobbie, 1947-
    China, the culture

(Lands, peoples, and cultures series)
Includes index.

ISBN 0-86505-209-3 (bound), ISBN 0-86505-289-1 (pbk.)
1. China - Social life and customs - Juvenile literature.
2. China - Civilization - Juvenile literature.
I. Kalman, Bobbie, 1947-   II. Series.

DS721.C5 1989   j951   LC 93-27370

Published by
Crabtree Publishing Company

350 Fifth Avenue	360 York Road, RR 4	73 Lime Walk
Suite 3308	Niagara-on-the-Lake	Headington,
New York	Ontario, Canada	Oxford OX3 7AD
N.Y. 10118	L0S 1J0	United Kingdom

Contents

The people of China have experienced a tremendous period of change in the last one hundred years. During this period of political turmoil they had little time or energy for cultural activities. Sometimes people were fighting in wars to save their country. At other times the government in power discouraged activities such as painting, dancing, playing music, and religious worship. At times people were punished for having an interest in arts that did not have government approval.

This new artist, Zhang Furong, draws on themes of folk art but uses western painting techniques.

In the last few years China's culture has experienced a revival. People are rediscovering their traditions. They are once again celebrating traditional festivals and practicing their chosen religions. Painters, musicians, and writers all over the country are busy creating new works. The people of China are experiencing a renewed love for their arts and a new pride in their culture.

(opposite, top left) With fifty-six national groups, China is truly a multicultural society. These Uygur children from the Xinjiang autonomous region are learning a traditional dance.

(above) Members of a local band practice playing their cymbals and drum for the Spring Festival.

(below) A troupe of young Shanghai acrobats perform for an enthusiastic audience in Beijing.

In the early days of history China's culture was more advanced than that of any other country. In those days Europeans had never seen creations such as the ones invented by the Chinese. Adventurers and merchants sailed to China to bring these treasured objects back to their countries. The clock, wheelbarrow, crossbow, compass, animal harness, porcelain, ink, the printing press, and playing cards are just a few of the inventions the resourceful Chinese have passed on to the rest of the world.

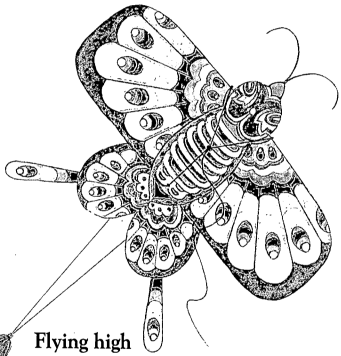

Flying high

Perhaps you love to fly a kite on windy days. The Chinese were the first people ever to fly kites. They are still such avid kite fans that a Kite Festival is held every year in April. On this day everyone climbs a hill or finds an open area for flying kites and having fun.

The Chinese are experts at making kites. They make colorful kites in the shapes of dragons, birds, butterflies, and centipedes. Some animal-shaped kites are designed so they can roll their eyes and flutter their wings. Other kites are so big that they require four or five people to operate them!

Mulberry bark paper

In ancient China written records were kept on strips of bamboo that were tied together. These documents were difficult to store because they took up too much room. In 105 A.D. Ts'ai Lun, an official with the imperial court, had an ingenious idea. He mixed together a mushy mixture of mulberry bark, hemp, rags, and old fish nets. He pressed the pulp into very thin sheets and allowed them to dry. The result was the first piece of paper!

Exploding bamboo

The first fireworks were made by stuffing gunpowder into hollow sticks of bamboo. Chinese medicine men probably discovered gunpowder while searching for cures. They adopted the use of gunpowder as a way to scare off evil spirits and ghosts. Today the tradition of lighting fireworks on holidays is still very popular in China. The loud bangs and pops of fireworks are believed to ensure good luck by scaring off bad spirits.

The compass

The Chinese were the first to discover that a magnetic object could indicate direction. The ancient Chinese used a special stone called a lodestone to locate suitable burial sites. In later days travelers used it to guide them in the right direction. The lodestone was eventually replaced by a magnetized needle in a device called a compass.

The abacus

In China both students and business people use the abacus for making calculations. An abacus is a hand-operated device that consists of rows of beads on metal rods set in a rectangular wooden frame. The Chinese invented this counting instrument in the second century B.C. Some Chinese are so skilled that they can figure out a problem on an abacus faster than someone using an electronic calculator!

Guarding the secret of silk

In earlier days European traders traveled all the way to China to buy a fine, smooth fabric called silk. For many years the Chinese kept the secret of silk production to themselves. They alone knew that silk was made from the cocoons of tiny silkworms. Western peoples eventually learned the secret of silk-making, but the Chinese are still famous for the quality and beauty of their silk fabrics.

How silk is made

Producing silk is a lengthy process. It takes forty thousand silkworms to produce just five-and-a-half kilograms of silk! The pictures on this page show the steps of silk-making. Match the information below to the pictures.

- After silkworm eggs are hatched in a warm room, baby worms feed on mulberry leaves until they are very fat. Thousands of feeding worms are kept on trays that are stacked one on top of another. A roomful of munching worms sounds like heavy rain falling on a roof.
- The silkworms feed until they have stored up enough energy to enter the cocoon stage. When it is time to build their cocoons, the worms produce a jelly-like substance in their silk glands, which hardens when it comes into contact with air. Silkworms spend three or four days spinning a cocoon around them-selves until they look like puffy, white balls.
- After eight or nine days in a warm, dry place the cocoons are ready to be unwound. First they are steamed or baked to kill the worms, or pupas. The cocoons are dipped into hot water to loosen the tightly woven strands. Then the strands are unwound onto a spool. Each cocoon is made up of a thread between 600 and 900 meters long! Between five and eight of these super-fine threads are twisted together to make one thread.
- Finally the silk threads are woven into cloth or used for embroidery work. Clothes made from silk are not only beautiful and lightweight, they are also warm in cool weather and cool in hot weather!

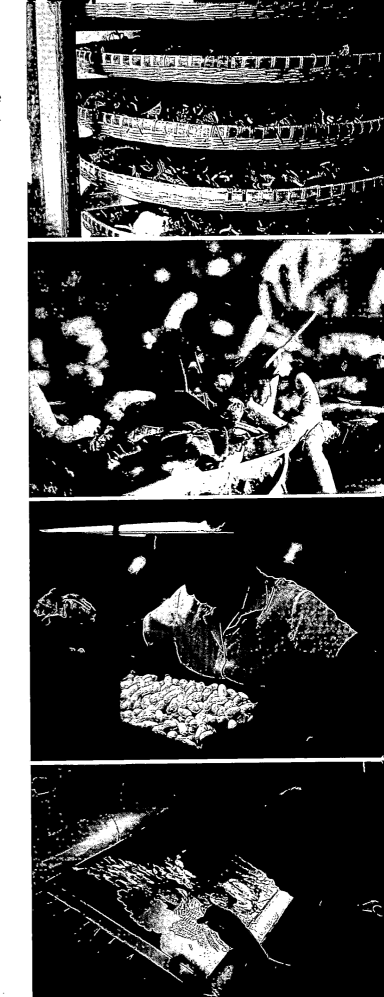

Traditional arts

The Chinese are famous for many of their traditional arts. From the earliest times Chinese craftspeople produced artworks of high quality. Painting and calligraphy, sculpture, architecture, and the creation of fine porcelain are just a few of the arts that date back almost as far as China itself. Many Chinese arts have been adopted by people all over the world.

The calligraphy of Confucius, Mao Zedong, and others are displayed on brass plates in museums. Tourists make rubbings of the plates as keepsakes.

Calligraphy

The art of fine writing is called calligraphy. The first great Chinese calligraphers lived sixteen hundred years ago. In these ancient times the Chinese people considered calligraphy to be the most beautiful art form. Artists were highly respected because it took great skill to master the difficult brushstrokes.

(above) Many historic buildings have painted ceilings and walls. The scene pictured above is from a ceiling panel at the Summer Palace near Beijing. What aspects of the scene make it obvious that the painting is very old?

Delicate brushstrokes

Calligraphy is still important in modern China. When children learn to read and write, they also learn calligraphy's delicate brushstrokes. The thousands of complicated pictographs that make up the Chinese alphabet are based on the eight brushstrokes of calligraphy.

Calligraphers often write out poems in fine script using black ink and brushes made from animal hair. Chinese writing is well suited to poetry because many of its pictographs resemble the idea they are communicating. For example, the character for "way" or "path" looks something like a foot striding forward, as if a person were actually walking down a path.

Painting

Traditional Chinese painting is based on the eight brushstrokes that are used in calligraphy. Many other brushstrokes are used as well, each with a special purpose. For example, a certain stroke is used for painting bamboo, another for trees, and one for rocks and mountains. Many Chinese paintings depict nature. Landscapes and symbolic birds and flowers are popular subjects.

These works of art are painted on long panels of paper or silk. Fans, screens, and wall and ceiling panels are also painted. A painted handscroll made of silk or paper is read by slowly unrolling the scroll for viewers to see. A poem often accompanies the painting to help people understand the meaning of the picture.

China's china

Pottery was one of the first crafts of ancient China. Originally it was made for everyday use. The finest of all pottery is porcelain, which the Chinese invented in the ninth century. Porcelain is made from a mixture of coal dust and a fine, white clay called kaolin. It is fired or baked at an extremely high temperature, more than 1200°C. Ordinary ceramics are fired at around 500°C. The piece is then glazed and fired again to make it shiny. This process makes a precious ceramic substance that is hard, thin, and translucent.

Plain, yet beautiful

Porcelain is naturally white or cream colored. The early pieces were left in this original state. Artists only began using dyes in the thirteenth century. A deep blue dye made from a mineral called cobalt was especially popular. This dye was used to create the beautiful blue-and-white vases made during the Ming dynasty, which have become famous all over the world.

A few centuries ago Chinese porcelain was in such great demand that merchants from many countries sailed to China to trade for it. It soon became known as china. Today people use this term, not only for porcelain, but for all kinds of dishes and pottery. Although most porcelain is now made in factories, much of it is still painted by hand.

A beautiful Ming vase

(opposite) A calligrapher's hand appears to dance gracefully as it paints Chinese characters.

Living rock

In ancient China the ability to sculpt was considered a skill rather than an art. Great sculptures were created to express religious devotion. Images of Buddha carved out of natural rock formations are among China's most spectacular works of art. Some of these carvings are as tall as five-story buildings. They are so lifelike that they certainly deserve the nickname "living rock!"

Thousands of Buddhas

In clusters of caves in northern China, thousands of images of Buddha have been carved into the cave walls. The oldest of these are the Dunhuang Caves in which dedicated monks carved Buddhas and painted the walls for over ten centuries. In the 492 caves there are more than two thousand sculptures of the Buddha and some fifty thousand square meters of beautiful religious wall paintings. The Yungang Grottoes near Datong contain the largest and most beautiful cave sculptures in China. Although many caves have been deteriorating, fifty-three of them survive, containing over fifty thousand images of the Buddha, angels, and animals, ranging from a few centimeters to over seventeen meters high. The pictures on this page show two walls of these carvings and paintings.

Traditional architecture

Although the Chinese civilization is thousands of years old, only a few ancient buildings are still standing. China's early buildings have not survived because nearly all of them were made of wood, which has decayed over time. Although stone was used for city walls, wood was used for homes and temples because the Chinese liked its natural qualities. The oldest building in China is a wooden temple built in the year 782.

The best place to view Chinese architecture is at historic sites. Colorful buildings with curved, upswept eaves, bright roof tiles, and carved adornments are all part of traditional Chinese architecture. The dragon, crane, phoenix, unicorn, and other symbols are painted or carved into the walls and roof supports. These animals symbolize good fortune and long life.

The way Chinese buildings are constructed is more symbolic than practical. Buildings face south because north is thought to be the source of evil. Red is used to bring good fortune, and yellow is the emperor's color. The number of steps or columns usually represents important things such as the four seasons of the year or the five virtues of Buddhism. Nine is the emperor's number. Western buildings are first planned by architects, but Chinese buildings are often planned with the help of advisors whose job it is to ensure that buildings will bring the best fortune to their future residents.

Pretty pagodas

Perhaps the building most symbolic of China is the pagoda, even though the design originally came from India. Pagodas look like several one-story buildings stacked one on top of another, with each story having its own roof. Some pagodas are square; others have many sides. Some are made of wood; others are of stone. The highest ones are the most sacred. Pagodas can be found at Buddhist temples and contain religious relics. They are not designed as dwellings. In fact, they usually have solid cores!

Chinese opera singers wear elaborate costumes and makeup. This character wears the villain's patch.

Performing arts

Amazing circus acrobats

Imagine trying to balance another person on your head while standing on top of a stack of ten chairs! Acrobats must be very agile and flexible to perform such stunts as spinning plates on tall poles or juggling while walking on a giant ball. For two thousand years professional Chinese acrobats have been performing tricks as difficult and spectacular as these. Today acrobatic and circus troupes continue to amaze audiences throughout China and around the world.

A night at the opera

The opera is a popular form of entertainment in China. Operas are at least three hours long. At one time they lasted up to three days! Although the songs in a Chinese opera may be hard to understand, even for a Chinese person, the viewer can still catch much of what is going on from the gestures, makeup, and costumes. A trembling body, for example, means fear, and crossed eyes show anger. The villain always has a white patch on his nose.

There are many different styles of opera, each one originating from a different region. Of all of the styles, the most famous is the Beijing Opera. It features high-pitched singing, elaborate costumes, and a large percussion section. Beijing operas are often based on historical events from imperial times.

Shadow puppets

Shadow-puppet shows are sometimes called the "opera of the common man." The stories are the same as those of the grand operas, but they are presented with only a few props. Puppeteers move their puppets between a bright light and a screen or sheet to create a shadow effect.

(opposite, top right) Many Chinese children dream about joining acrobatic troupes.

(opposite, bottom) Circus acrobats dressed in colorful lion costumes perform to the music of drums, cymbals, gongs, and bells.

Chinese music

Since 1949 very little music was played in China. Then, ten years ago, the Chinese government started encouraging people to take up cultural activities such as music once again. Although western music is very popular in China now, the Chinese have also become interested in their traditional music. The Conservatory of Chinese Music and other schools have begun training musicians in this art. People all over China are attending concerts in which typical Chinese instruments, such as the *hu qin*, the *pipa* lute, and *sheng* pipes, are played.

The main instrument in the Chinese orchestra is the *hu qin*. It has two strings and is played with a bow. The *pipa* lute has more strings and is plucked like a guitar. Many children are learning to play the *pipa*. Chinese flutes, such as the *xiao*, are made of bamboo. The most traditional Chinese instrument is the *sheng* pipe, which is made of several bamboo reeds.

After school, children learn how to play the pipa.

Chinese cuisine

The art of Chinese cooking is both ancient and colorful. It is known for its variety of flavors and textures and by its many different cooking styles. Steaming and stir-frying are the most common ways to cook food in China. Besides these, there are some eighty other cooking techniques. Chinese chefs are so highly regarded for their cooking skills that they are sometimes called "doctors of food."

Fresh and fast

Chinese food is prepared with the freshest ingredients. Bite-sized pieces cook quickly and can be easily eaten with chopsticks. Stir-frying food in a wok is one of the most popular cooking methods. Only a small amount of oil is needed in this deep, round frying pan. Stir-frying food in hot oil not only preserves the nutritional value of the food, it saves fuel as well! Great attention is paid to the colors and presentation of the food.

Chinese cooking is famous for its lack of waste. Whether from land or sea, almost every type and part of an animal is eaten, including eel, sea slug, snake, jellyfish, chicken feet, and duck tongues. Imaginative names are also characteristic of Chinese cuisine. Eight-jewel Duck, Red-cooked Lion's Head, and Gold Coin are just a few examples of Chinese dishes.

Stir-frying in a wok requires very little oil.

Regional cooking styles

There are five major schools of Chinese cooking: Canton, Fukien, Honan, Sichuan, and Shantung. The Cantonese style originates from the region around Guangzhou (once known as Canton) and is the most familiar to Westerners. Dishes such as egg rolls, chop suey, and chow mein are all part of Cantonese cooking. A mild climate and access to the sea give the chefs of this area a wide variety of ingredients from which to choose. Cantonese cooks follow the Daoist principle, which teaches that food should be eaten as near to its natural state as possible. It should be fresh and cooked only for a short time.

Fukien, Honan, and Sichuan

The province of Fukien has a long sea coast, so a wide variety of seafood is available to its residents. Fukien cuisine is well known for its delicate flavors and clear soups. Cooks of Honan were the first to produce the famous Chinese sweet-and-sour sauce and the deep-fried method of cooking. This province in southwestern China is known for spicy foods that can set your mouth on fire! Sichuan dishes are made with red-chili and peppercorn pastes, fermented rice, and brown sugar. The result is hot, sweet, and sour flavors.

Eels are just one of the many varieties of food sold at the local market.

Shantung

Shantung is the northernmost of all the different schools of cooking. It is best known for duck soup and Peking Duck. Peking Duck is a delicacy that comes from Beijing, which used to be known as Peking. The waiter announces the arrival of this fabulous dish at the table by striking a gong. Flavorings such as soya sauce, garlic, and black and red bean pastes are also popular. Little rice is farmed in the north, so wheat noodles and dumplings serve as the northern residents' staple starchy foods. They particularly enjoy lamb dishes.

The Mongolian Hot Pot

The Mongolian Hot Pot came to China during the time the Mongols ruled the country. It is a famous northern fondue-style dish that is centered around a pot filled with boiling soup stock. A variety of raw meat is arranged in dishes around the pot. The diners cook their own meals by dipping pieces of meat into the boiling broth. The meat cooks quickly and adds flavor to the boiling stock. Several sauces, such as hot mustard, peanut, and soya, go with the meat. After the diners have finished their meat, they drink the flavorful broth to which vegetables such as spinach and cabbage have been added.

(circle) Diners use chopsticks to dip their meat into the Mongolian Hot Pot and accompanying sauces.

Eating Chinese-style

The classic Chinese table is round to allow guests to be at an equal distance from the food. Each place setting has bowls, a china spoon, sauces, and chopsticks. Dishes are brought in one at a time, and the diners serve themselves from a platter. When eating with chopsticks, you should remember two things: never to touch your mouth with the chopsticks and not to cross your chopsticks when you have finished your meal. Both of these actions are considered bad manners. For a lesson on how to use chopsticks, see page 30.

All the tea in China

No Chinese meal is complete without a pot of hot tea. In fact, the Chinese introduced the rest of the world to this popular beverage. Tea is still a very important part of Chinese culture. It is sipped at every meal, offered to all guests, and served in local teahouses. It is believed to have a calming effect, and some herbal teas serve medicinal purposes. The Chinese prepare tea by pouring boiling water over loose tea leaves. The flavorful brew is drunk without milk or sugar from small cups without handles. Chinese teas come in all kinds of colors and flavors, such as green, yellow, red, mint, and flower-blossom.

Outdoor restaurants serve simple but tasty foods.

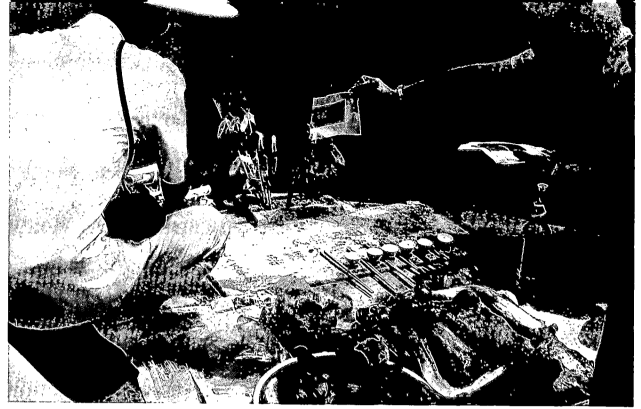

Old and new beliefs

Chinese folk religion is filled with gods, demons, and spirits. Many of China's traditional festivals are based on ancient myths about these super-natural creatures. Old practices, such as offering gifts to the gods, are part of Chinese folk religion. The Chinese also worship their ancestors, who are believed to possess the power to help or hinder the lives of their living descendants.

Yin and *Yang*

Many Chinese believe that the universe is made up of two forces: *yin* and *yang*. *Yin* is feminine and *yang* is masculine. *Yin* and *yang* are opposites that work together to create a balance. Examples of *yin* are characteristics such as soft, right, and cold. These are balanced out by the *yang* qualities of hard, left, and warm. The well-being of the world, the body, and the soul are believed to depend on these forces staying in balance.

The teachings of Confucius

Although the Chinese believed in a variety of gods, it was two men, Confucius and Lao Zi, who introduced the principles by which many

people lived. Confucius was a scholar who lived from 551 to 479 B.C. According to Confucius the ideal person was polite, honest, courageous, and wise. For more than two thousand years Chinese society was based on the Confucian code of behavior. Children were taught to obey their parents, and everyone was expected to respect the elderly and obey the rulers of the country.

Lao Zi and Daoism

Daoism is also very old. It is based on a short book written by a man known as Lao Zi, who lived around the same time as Confucius. Daoists believe that achieving the balance of the *yin* and *yang* is the key to achieving spiritual peace. Daoism teaches the importance of harmony with nature and encourages a simple way of life. Although neither Confucianism nor Daoism is widely practiced as religions today, both have deeply affected the characters of the Chinese people.

The yin *and* yang *contain the seeds of each other.*

(top) Family members burn flame papers and offer food to honor the memory of their ancestors.

A sculpture of a laughing, well-fed Buddha

(top) Lama Buddhist monks chant to the beat of drums and bells.

Buddhism

There was once a man named Sakyamuni who lived in India. One day, while meditating, he discovered that good would be rewarded with good, and evil with evil. He became the Buddha, which means the "Awakened One." Those who follow the teachings of Buddha believe that people are born over and over again in higher or lower states as human beings, animals, or insects. If you live a life of good deeds, your next life will be a good one. But if you live a life of evil, your next life is sure to be full of suffering and misfortune.

Buddhism was brought to China from India in the fifth century B.C. Over the years China has developed its own version called Chan Buddhism, also known as Zen Buddhism, a mix of Daoist and Buddhist beliefs. Tibetans and Mongols practice another version of Buddhism called Lama Buddhism.

Islam and Christianity

In China there are fewer Muslims and Christians than Buddhists. The Islamic religion was founded at Mecca, Saudi Arabia, by a prophet named Muhammed. It was brought to China by Arab traders in the seventh century. The Kazaks and Uygurs who live in the western regions follow the Islamic faith. Christianity, which is based on the teachings of Jesus Christ, came to China in the sixteenth century. European missionaries introduced it to the Chinese.

New freedom

When China became a communist country in 1949, the Chinese were not allowed to practice any religion. Then in 1982 the Chinese government declared that all citizens were once again allowed religious freedom. Temples, monasteries, and churches are being restored after years of being used for housing, factory space, and storage.

unicorn

phoenix

Chinese symbols

Over the centuries the Chinese have created many symbols to express the values that are important to them. Signs, colors, and even animals symbolize such things as long life, happiness, peace, and beauty.

Shou — The *shou* sign was adapted from the Chinese character or pictograph that means long life. It appears everywhere—sewn onto silk, carved in jade, and painted on porcelain.

Fu — The sign for happiness also comes from the Chinese language. The character *fu* is often surrounded by bats because *fu* also means bat.

Dragon — The dragon is a symbol representing the country of China, but it also has other meanings. According to ancient Chinese legend, the imaginary dragon was the god of rain. When he breathed, he produced the clouds. In spring he brought the rain; in winter he buried himself in the mud at the bottom of the sea. He is a symbol of spring and new life.

Phoenix — The phoenix is an imaginary bird that looks something like a peacock. It is a symbol of beauty, peace, the summer harvest, and long life. When pictured together, the dragon and phoenix foretell good luck, so they are often used as wedding decorations.

Unicorn — The Chinese unicorn looks different from the ones you may have seen in pictures. The unicorn is a Buddhist symbol of wisdom, so it is sometimes shown carrying a law book.

Tortoise — The tortoise is a symbol of the universe. Its round back represents the sky, and its belly the earth. The tortoise is a symbol of strength and long life because it was believed to live for a thousand years.

Lion — Sculptures of lions are often placed as guards outside important buildings. A male lion is usually shown playing with a ball. A female lion has a tiny cub under her paw. What gender is the lion in the photograph?

shou, *the sign of long life*

fu, *the sign of happiness*

The Chinese horoscope

In western astrology a person's fortune is predicted by observing the location of the stars and planets on the day of his or her birth. Instead of the birth day, the ancient Chinese horoscope predicts that people born in a certain year have a particular set of characteristics.

Animal characteristics

A Chinese legend explains that all the animals of the world were invited to come and visit the Buddha. Only twelve animals came. In order to reward these animals for their loyalty, the Buddha named a year after each one in the order they appeared before him. The cycle of animal names repeats every twelve years. The people born in the year of a certain animal are believed to have some of the characteristics of that animal. For instance, if you were born in 1982, the year of the dog, you may have a deep sense of loyalty and duty, just as a dog is thought to have! Look at the following chart to see what traits you, your friends, parents, and teachers have. What characteristics would you add to the list to describe your personality?

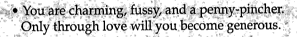

Your year	Are these your traits?
Year of the Rat 1948, 1960, 1972, 1984	• You are charming, fussy, and a penny-pincher. Only through love will you become generous.
Year of the Ox 1949, 1961, 1973, 1985	• You are quiet and patient until angered. You inspire confidence. You are also stubborn.
Year of the Tiger 1950, 1962, 1974, 1986	• You are courageous. Sometimes you are selfish. Though sympathetic, you can be suspicious.
Year of the Rabbit 1951, 1963, 1975, 1987	• You are fortunate and well-respected. Sometimes you are a daydreamer.
Year of the Dragon 1952, 1964, 1976, 1988	• You are healthy, energetic, short tempered, and stubborn. You are honest and brave.
Year of the Snake 1953, 1965, 1977, 1989	• You are quiet and wise and like to dress up. You help other people but tend to overdo it.
Year of the Horse 1942, 1954, 1966, 1978	• You are independent. You talk too much. You are popular, but sometimes you trust the wrong people.
Year of the Sheep 1943, 1955, 1967, 1979	• You are gentle in your ways. Sometimes you are pessimistic. You are a very cultured person.
Year of the Monkey 1944, 1956, 1968, 1980	• You are a genius, but you are not steady. Though clever and skillful, you can be impatient.
Year of the Rooster 1945, 1957, 1969, 1981	• Only sometimes are you fortunate. You work hard, but you often take on too much.
Year of the Dog 1946, 1958, 1970, 1982	• You have a deep sense of loyalty and duty. Your tongue is sharp, but you keep secrets well.
Year of the Boar 1947, 1959, 1971, 1983	• You are brave and can do anything you decide to do. You have few friends, but they last for life.

19

Colorful and noisy parades

In China many of the festivals today are connected with national celebrations. Labor Day, Women's Day, Children's Day, and Army Day are just a few of these. The two most important celebrations in modern China are Liberation Day and Chinese New Year.

Liberation Day

On October 1, 1949, Mao Zedong announced the founding of the People's Republic of China. Every year since then the Chinese celebrate Liberation Day on October 1. This day is the biggest national holiday in China. Thousands of people from all over the country gather in Beijing to celebrate this occasion. One can meet farmers and factory workers from near and far, Mongols in long sheepskin coats, and Tibetans in embroidered waistcoats. Everybody takes part in a huge parade on Qang Street. They wave banners and march past the Gate of Heavenly Peace. After the parade everyone goes to the park in the Forbidden City for fireworks, singing, and dancing.

Spring Festival

Rather than on January first, Chinese New Year falls in early spring. The Chinese used to follow a calendar that was based on the cycles of the moon. Unlike the solar calendar, which divides the year into twelve months, the ancient Chinese calendar had thirteen months. For this reason, the Chinese New Year, also known as the Spring Festival, is held on the first day of the first lunar month, which occurs at the end of January or beginning of February.

An ancient Chinese legend says that a long time ago, there was a monster who ate people. The gods decided to lock him up inside a mountain to protect the population from being devoured. Once a year, however, during New Year, the gods allowed him to come out. The Chinese kept him away from their homes by lighting firecrackers. The monster was frightened away by the flashing and banging. This bright, noisy display has become a tradition at midnight every New Year.

Making preparations

Spring Festival is a big celebration, and everyone prepares for the event well in advance. People begin by setting up an altar for Zao Wang, the lord of the stove. At one time a picture of Zao Wang hung by the kitchen stove in every home. People believed that he went up to heaven during the Spring Festival and reported to the gods about each household. If the report was good, the gods would look after the family throughout the rest of the year. To make sure Zao Wang had sweet things to say, the Chinese spread honey on his mouth! Before the New Year arrives, the Chinese try to pay back debts and rid their hearts of grudges.

A family time

During Spring Festival families visit the tombs of their dead relatives. They honor their ancestors by lighting incense and burning imitation money. Afterwards, everyone goes back to their homes for a huge feast, the best dinner of the whole year. Children are given presents of money, and their parents let them stay up late.

A lion dancer prepares for the Spring Festival.

(top and opposite top) National festivals such as Liberation Day are celebrated with colorful parades.

Dancing dragons

On the third day of the Spring Festival the Chinese have a parade of dragon and lion dancers. The dragon costume has a papier mâché head and a long, colorful, sequin-covered body. The dragon is so huge, it takes two people to hold up his head and twelve more to act as his legs. The streets are crowded and noisy during the parade, and there is a constant banging of firecrackers. As the dragon passes everyone's home, people open their doors to let in the good luck that the dragon brings. Some people write rhymes in their best calligraphy and hang them on their doorways.

In China people celebrate many festivals that date back to ancient times. Although many traditional festivals were replaced by national ones in 1949, many people in rural areas continued to celebrate in the old ways. Most traditional festivals correspond to important dates on the old Chinese calendar.

There are fifty-six national groups in China, all with their own cultures and celebrations. Some of these groups take part in the traditional Chinese festivals, adding their customs to the celebrations. They may dress in traditional costumes, play special instruments, or perform local folk dances.

Harvest Moon Festival

Food is important to every person, so celebrating the harvest is one of the most important holidays around the world. It is no different in China. The Chinese celebrate this special time of thanksgiving with the Harvest Moon Festival.

On the evening of the Harvest Moon Festival people climb hills and mountains to get a good view of the full moon. They carry fish- and bird-shaped paper lanterns. They give thanks for the harvest to the bright full moon of the eighth lunar month. Sometimes people also burn moon papers. Moon papers have pictures of rabbits and toads on them. According to Chinese mythology, a rabbit and a three-legged toad live on the moon. They are the moon's companions.

Sweet moon cakes

Friends and relatives give each other mouth-watering pastries called moon cakes. These small cakes contain a variety of sweet stuffings, such as red bean paste, almond paste, or eggs. They are baked in molds, and an egg-yolk glaze gives them a shiny look. They often have flower or leaf designs on the top. Moon cakes are always piled thirteen high—one cake for every lunar month of the Chinese calendar.

An old legend recounts how moon cakes once saved the Chinese. A long time ago China was ruled by foreigners. The Chinese wanted to get rid of them. At the Harvest Moon Festival they hid messages inside moon cakes and passed them around to let everyone know of a secret plan of attack. At the arranged time, they got together and overthrew their cruel rulers.

A Miao musician celebrates a festival wearing a fancy feather headdress. He accompanies traditional Miao folk dancers with a tune played on a type of sheng pipe.

Harvest moon cookies

Harvest moon cakes are very difficult to make, but you can make our version of harvest moon cookies instead! Here are the ingredients you will need for the cookie dough:

    250 mL (1 cup) softened butter
    125 mL (1/2 cup) icing sugar
    10 mL (2 tsp) vanilla
    250 mL (1 cup) ground blanched almonds
    375 mL (1 1/2 cups) sifted all-purpose flour

Cream butter with big spoon. Sift sugar and gradually mix with the butter. Blend in vanilla and almonds, and slowly knead in flour. Put dough into refrigerator.

The fun part

Once the dough has cooled, it is ready for rolling. Sprinkle some flour on your rolling pin and on the kitchen counter. Roll out your dough to a thickness of one centimeter. Now you can cut or form it into shapes! An upside-down glass works well as a full-moon-shaped cookie cutter. Make a crescent-shaped moon by cutting a full moon into two halves and pulling at the two ends until it looks like a crescent shape. To make a rabbit or a toad, cut the shapes out on a piece of paper, press the paper down on the rolled-out dough, and trim around the shape. Bake the cookies on a greased cookie sheet in a preheated 180°C (350°F) oven for fifteen minutes.

23

The Lantern Festival

The Lantern Festival comes two weeks after the Spring Festival. During this celebration people carry candlelit lanterns shaped like goldfish, birds, and red globes through the streets. Rows of lanterns floating in the darkness is a spectacular sight. Sometimes groups of children act out a play or perform a lantern dance.

Qing Ming Festival

The Qing Ming Festival takes place in April. It is a time when Chinese people honor the dead. In the past people tended the graves of deceased relatives with great care. They spent the day pulling weeds, planting flowers, and sweeping around the grave sites. The family then shared a picnic lunch and burned sticks of incense in honor of their ancestors. The festival has changed over the years. Now this day honors those who fought and died in the revolutionary war.

Festival of Ice and Snow

In the middle of winter in Harbin the temperatures can fall below -30°C. Residents of this northern Chinese city have a yearly festival to help them forget about the cold weather. They make huge ice sculptures with names such as "Moon Palace" and "Vivid Pagoda." Ice lanterns are made by hollowing out a block of ice and putting a candle inside. They are used to light up the sculptures at night.

The Dragon Boat Festival

The Dragon Boat Festival is celebrated on rivers in southern China. It is connected with the death of the politician and poet Qu Yuan. In 288 B.C. Qu Yuan ended his life by throwing himself into the Miluo River in Yunan Province to protest the corrupt government. People respected Qu Yuan and wanted to find him and give him a proper funeral and burial. They launched their boats into the river and threw rice overboard to distract the fish from his body while they searched for him.

Today people eat pyramid-shaped rice cakes and race beautiful boats shaped like dragons to honor Qu Yuan's memory. Dragon boats are long and slim, sometimes over twenty-seven meters long. The prow is carved in the shape of a huge dragon head and the hull is beautifully painted. As many as seventy rowers are needed to power each boat. Everyone in the audience shouts for his or her favorite racing team. The spectators clang cymbols and gongs and wave colorful flags. The dragon boat race is a very noisy and exciting festival!

Seventy rowers speed towards the finish line as the sternsman quickens his shouts of "Row! row! row!" The crowd cheers the crew on to success with cymbals, gongs, and colorful flags.

Although the Chinese practice modern western medicine, they also depend on traditional Chinese methods. These ancient healing techniques are based on six thousand years of practical experience. Patients are treated with medicinal herbs, acupuncture, exercise, massage, and cupping.

Restoring the balance

The Chinese believe that most illness is caused by an interruption in the *qi*, which is the vital energy of the body. Just as the *yin* and *yang* create a balance in the universe, these forces must also be balanced in the body so that the *qi* can flow properly. When the body is out of balance, a person becomes ill. A person with too much heat in his or her body, for example, might suffer from boils. Since heat is caused by the *yang*, the doctor will prescribe a *yin* remedy such as dandelions, which have a cooling effect. Thus the balance of *yin* and *yang* is restored. Many Chinese people still trust this method of treatment over modern techniques.

Herbs and "dragon bones"

Treatment with medicinal herbs is the most popular kind of traditional Chinese medicine. There are many types of herbs. A well-stocked herbalist carries up to six thousand folk remedies! Wood, bark, and ten types of ginseng root are used as herbal-tea ingredients. Ground-up animal parts, such as sea shells and fossilized bones and teeth, known as "dragon bones," are also used as remedies.

Cures that kill animals

Each year many animals are hunted and killed because their parts are used in traditional Chinese remedies. Thousands of animals must be killed to meet the yearly demand for Chinese medical supplies. Some herbalists sell bear paws and spleens, rhinoceros horns, deer antlers, and sea horses for medicinal purposes. Some of these animals belong to endangered species. Hunters sometimes even kill pandas by

accident while trying to trap other animals. There are only a thousand pandas left in the world! Poachers also hunt the rhinoceros, deer, tiger, and bear in other parts of the world such as Africa, India, and Canada. This practice angers many people!

The mystery of acupuncture

Acupuncture is an ancient way of treating illness by stimulating certain "pressure points." Very fine, sterilized needles are painlessly inserted at key points on the body. Stimulating these points is said to restore the patient's *qi* to its normal balance. Western doctors are not exactly sure how acupuncture works, but they know it does!

Acupuncture is used to cure ailments, relieve pain, and anesthetize patients for surgery. When acupuncture is used as an anesthetic, patients remain awake throughout the operation and can even talk to the doctor. Since patients do not have to recover from any side effects, they can often leave the operating room by themselves!

Cupping

Cupping is another traditional technique used by Chinese doctors. Bamboo cups are immersed in hot water and are then applied to the body at acupuncture points. When the cup is put on the skin, the hot air inside cools and contracts, creating suction. The skin swells up into the cup as the blood beneath the surface rushes into the small surface vessels. Cupping is believed to relieve the congestion caused by asthma, bronchitis, and the aches and pains that accompany rheumatism.

(circle, opposite) A patient receives a cupping treatment she hopes will relieve the discomfort of an asthma attack.

(opposite) Herbalists stock thousands of different kinds of roots, flowers, herbs, bark, and animal products. They get these from the surrounding countryside and special suppliers.

Barefoot doctors

Barefoot doctors are not doctors without shoes. They are rural paramedics who are qualified to treat minor medical problems. They also educate people about health and personal hygiene. Barefoot doctors were once part-time rice farmers who worked in the fields in their bare feet, just like the other farmers. Now they are trained in both western and traditional medical techniques and work full time in clinics and country hospitals.

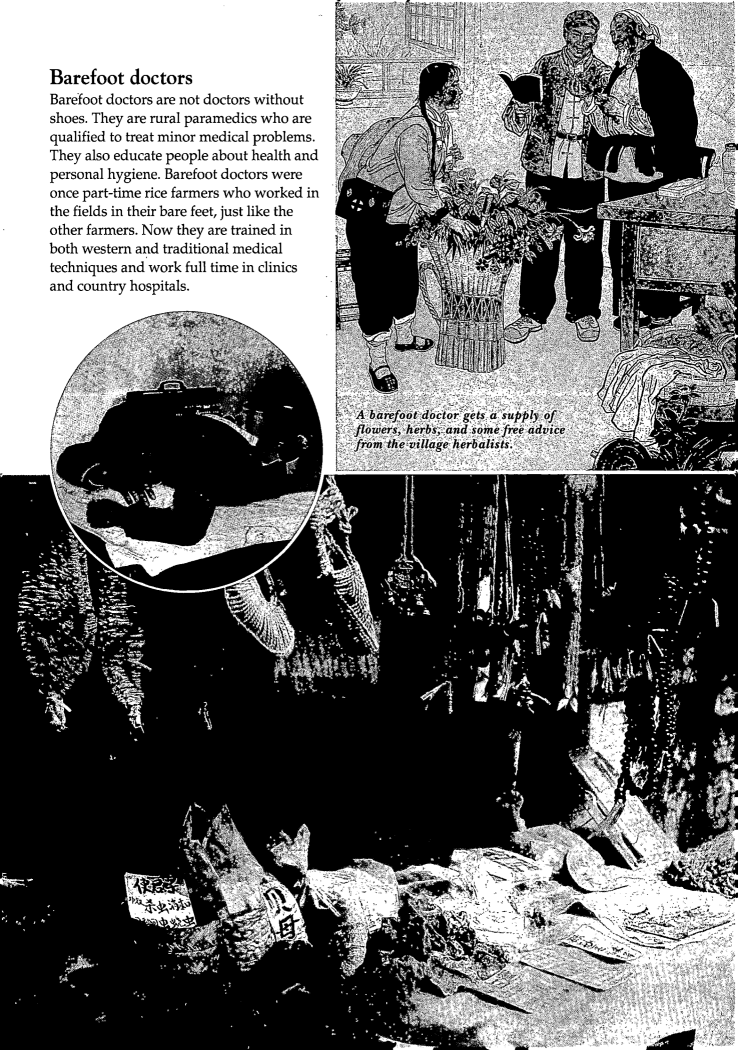

A barefoot doctor gets a supply of flowers, herbs, and some free advice from the village herbalists.

The Chinese are passionate about their hobbies. Clusters of friends gather in the streets and parks to discuss their favorite pastimes. They might be stamp collectors, comparing and trading their treasures, or pet owners admiring one another's animals. Many people can also be seen playing a variety of traditional games.

Mah jong

Mah jong is a popular adult game. People play it with great enthusiasm. *Mah jong* is very similar to four-handed Gin Rummy, but it has a set of 136 tiles rather than fifty-two cards. Instead of hearts, diamonds, spades, and clubs, *mah jong* tiles are decorated with bamboo, circles, and characters. The sound of *mah jong* being played is as distinctive as the game itself. The loud clicking of tiles being moved furiously around the table top is a familiar noise to every *mah jong* player.

Chinese chess and checkers

Chinese chess is not the same as international chess. Like international chess, Chinese chess is played on a board and involves "taking" the opponent's pieces, but there are no knights, kings, or queens. Chinese chess is an ancient game that uses flat, round, black and white stones on a grid-patterned board. The Chinese watch large national chess tournaments with keen interest. They also have their own version of checkers played on a star-shaped board.

Children's games

Do you like playing hopscotch, marbles, ping pong or Cat's Cradle? Many children in China do as well! They meet after school to play all sorts of games. One game, called Five Stones, is similar to Jacks. Children also like to skip rope and draw pictures on the cement with chalk.

(top) Chinese checkers is played all over the world.

A girl plays ti jian zi *with a pompom. After this first throw, she must keep the bag in the air by hitting it with her ankles, knees, and thighs.*

Fancy footwork

Another popular children's game is Kick-the-Bag. To play this game, a little bag is sewn together and filled with sand or grain. Then it is thrown into the air and kept there by kicking it with the inside of the heel. Kick-the-Bag can be played by one person or with others in a small circle. Another version of this game is called *ti jian zi*. Children find something light, such as a cork or a coin with a hole, and attach a feather to it for balance. They try to keep it in the air following rules similar to those of Kick-the-Bag. This game is far more difficult than it looks!

"Small games"

One of the best-loved hobbies in China is called "small games," or keeping pets. You may have a cat or a dog, but in China very few families would have such a big animal for a pet. Cats and dogs eat too much meat! Instead, Chinese people keep pigeons, singing birds, goldfish, and even crickets! Both children and adults take their pet hobbies very seriously.

A pet or a pest?

In China crickets have been pets for thousands of years. Women at the imperial palace used to keep them in golden cages! Now, instead of golden cages, people use little bamboo baskets for their crickets. In winter the owner puts a tiny hot-water bottle inside the cage to keep the cricket warm and happy. Not only are crickets easy to feed, they are also easy to carry along in a pocket—and as an added bonus, crickets sing, too!

Champion crickets

Some owners take their crickets to fighting matches that attract large audiences. Everybody watches as the crickets are placed in a wooden bowl. A bowl is used as the fighting ring because the crickets cannot cling to the sides. To begin the match, the crickets are tickled with a hair on the end of a tiny stick. Everyone gets very excited and cheers for his or her favorite dueling cricket. Can you guess how a cricket wins the match?

Caring for caged songbirds is a favorite hobby of elderly Chinese men.

Feathered friends

Many Chinese keep birds as pets. Elderly men often bring their songbirds to the park and hang their cages in the trees so their pets can be near other birds. It is delightful to hear all the birds sing together.

Some people keep pigeons. Owners attach homemade whistles to their pigeons' tails. As the birds fly through the air, the wind causes the whistles to blow. People with many pigeons give each one a different-sounding whistle. When the whole flock takes flight, it sounds like a symphony of flying whistles!

☯ Try these activities ☯

Papercutting

The ancient tradition of papercutting is still used to decorate countless Chinese homes today. This folk art involves cutting complicated shapes out of colored paper. You can make your own Chinese papercut by using materials in your home. Scissors, glue, and several sheets of brightly colored paper are the supplies that you will need. Draw a simple design, such as a snowflake, on the back of a colored sheet of paper. Carefully snip out the shapes, and then turn the paper over. Paste the papercut down on a white piece of paper, let it dry, and then hang it up. Now try more complicated designs, such as that shown at the top of this page or the one at the bottom of the opposite one. If you use red paper, the Chinese would say that good luck will soon come your way!

Wood and potato cuts

The traditional Chinese woodcut was used to capture images of beauty and peace. Woodcuts are made by engraving a design on one side of a wooden block. The carved side is coated with ink and pressed onto paper. The imprint of the woodblock design can be repeated over and over again by coating the woodcut with fresh ink each time.

Carving wood can be difficult. It requires special skill and the use of sharp woodworking tools. You can achieve a woodcut effect by carving a potato with a peeler or plastic knife.

Cut a potato in half and carve a design into the surface. Remember to cut away all the flat area around your design. When you have finished your cutting, fill the bottom of a pie plate with watercolor paint. Dip the potato into the paint and make a print on a piece of paper. Make other potato-print designs and combine them to make more complicated patterns.

Eating with chopsticks

Instead of using a knife and fork for eating, the Chinese use chopsticks. Look at the diagram to see how to work your new utensils. One chopstick is held between the thumb and the ring finger, and it never moves. The other chopstick is held by the tip of the thumb and the index and middle fingers. Remember to keep the tips even. It may seem very difficult the first time you try but, with practice, it will become easy. In China even the smallest children use chopsticks!

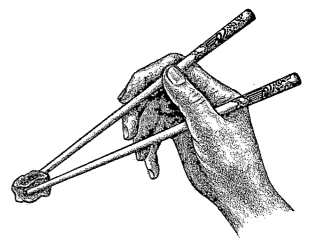

Your own Chinese opera

Create a Chinese opera in your classroom or with your neighborhood friends. Decide on a story based on a historical, school, or neighborhood event. Write an outline of the story and decide which parts you and your friends will play.

Chinese operas include singing, dancing, acrobatics, and pantomime. The actors learn both their lines and gestures. Colors are important, too. Red stands for loyalty, black for boldness, and white for evil. There is almost no improvisation in a Chinese opera.

Costumes, makeup, gestures

Devise a set of costume and makeup clues. Remember that in a real Chinese opera, costumes help identify the characters and makeup tells whether a character is good or evil, brave or fearful. Movements of the sleeves, arms and hands can give the setting for your story. For example, outstretched arms show that it is dark. You can invent five or ten different settings, such as: bent left elbow to show morning, or outstretched fingers to indicate schooltime. Be sure to share these clues with your audience so they can participate in your story. Perhaps you can get them to shout out words such as "schooltime," or "nighttime," when a setting has changed.

Your performance

Once you have a basic outline for your performance, you can let the characters fill in their own dialogue and create their own gestures. Make sure all the players learn their parts. Use dramatic and exaggerated actions. Prance and gallop. Pirrouette and pussyfoot. Let everyone have a turn bellowing and squealing, hitting high and low notes.

In Chinese opera sleeve movements and arm positions have specific meanings. What might this gesture mean?

You can stay in the opera mood at home by telling your parents about your school day in song instead of speech. Get your whole family to participate at dinner. They can sing, "Pass the peas, please!" with great flourish.

Improvise and have fun!

After having put on a structured Chinese-style opera, you may want to give another performance using your own style of opera. This time, do not learn lines. Improvise instead. Make your own set of rules and get dramatic!

Glossary

acupuncture - A way of treating illness by stimulating certain "pressure points" on the body

ancestors - People from whom one is descended

astrology - The study of the positions of stars and planets and their influence on people's lives

bronchitis - An illness caused by an infection of the tiny tubes in the lungs

calligraphy - The art of fine handwriting

cobalt - A metallic substance used to make a deep-blue dye

Confucius - An ancient Chinese scholar whose ideas have greatly influenced Chinese society for centuries

culture - The customs, beliefs, and arts of a distinct group of people. Culture also means the result of an interest in literature, history, and fine arts.

Daoism - A religion based on the teachings of Lao Zi, an ancient Chinese philosopher

endangered - Very close to becoming extinct, or no longer existing as a species

flame papers - Small square papers that are burned to honor ancestors

hemp - A strong plant fiber used to make rope

hull - The bottom and sides of a ship

incense - A substance that produces a sweet-smelling smoke when burned

lodestone - A type of iron ore that is naturally magnetized and can be used to indicate direction

lunar - Relating to the moon

Mao Zedong - Founder of the Chinese Communist Party and China's leader for twenty-seven years

Miao - One of China's fifty-six national groups who live in Guizhou province

missionaries - People sent by a church to spread their religion to those who do not yet believe in it

Mongol - One of China's fifty-six national groups, who live in the autonomous region of Inner Mongolia

myth - A legend or story that tries to explain mysterious events or ideas

national group - People who share a common background and lifestyle

pagoda - A type of building that looks like several one-story buildings stacked one on top of another

paramedic - A trained medical worker capable of performing basic medical procedures

percussion - Relating to musical instruments that require striking

pictograph - A picture used to represent a word

porcelain - A type of pottery made from a mixture of rock minerals and a fine, white clay

prophet - A religious leader believed to be inspired by God or a spirit

prow - The front part of a boat

relic - Something or a piece of something that has survived from the past

rheumatism - A painful condition that causes swollen and stiff muscles, bones, joints, and nerves

rural - Relating to the countryside

sculpture - The art of making figures by carving materials such as rock, wood, or ice

solar - Relating to the the sun

spleen - An oval-shaped organ near the stomach that filters the blood

symbol - Something that represents or stands for something else

traditional - Describing long-held customs or beliefs

universe - All that exists, including the earth, the sky, and outer space

western - The term used to describe people from the western part of the world, especially Europe and North America, as opposed to people from Asia, such as the Chinese and Japanese

Index

56789 WP Printed in the U.S.A. 8765